THE C

Artlist Collectiʊn

WHY DO CATS PURR?
And Other True Facts

By Apple Jordan

SCHOLASTIC INC.

New York   Toronto   London   Auckland   Sydney
Mexico City   New Delhi   Hong Kong   Buenos Aires

ISBN-13: 978-0-545-00088-8
ISBN-10: 0-545-00088-2

12 11 10 9 8 7 6 5 4 3 2 1   7 8 9 10 11 12/0

Printed in the U.S.A.
First printing, January 2007

# The Cat's Meow

We cats are a mysterious breed. Some of us are fussy and finicky. Some of us are cute and cuddly. Some of us are unsocial and downright snooty. We know we sometimes leave you bewildered by our baffling behavior. We scratch . . . we hiss . . . we eat grass, then have the nerve to turn up our noses at our dinner plates. And yet you still love us!

That's why we owe it to you to set the record straight — to answer your questions and give you the *cat's meow* on why we do the kooky things we do.

# Why do cats purr?

Purring is a rumbling sound we cats make deep down in our throats. It's our way of letting you know we're as happy as clams—or rather, cats. And why shouldn't we be? We're well fed, well loved, and well cared for. So all we have to do is sit back and *purr, purr, purr.*

Petting our fur is a good way to get us to purr. We like that a lot. And if we roll on our backs and show you our bellies that means we think you're the cat's pajamas. We may playfully swat at your hands with our claws while you're petting us. Don't worry—we're usually just play fighting! So keep up the good work of keeping your pussycat pleased. We know it's not always an easy job to do!

Feline Fact

Small cats are the only ones that purr. Big cats such as leopards and lions can only roar.

Why do cats meow?

That's an easy one . . . because we have a lot to say! Meowing is our way of communicating with humans. We meow to let you know how we feel and what we want. And do we want a lot! To be petted . . . to be fed . . . to play . . . to be fed . . . to be let in . . . to be fed . . . And if you listen to us closely, you'll be able to tell which meow means what. That would save us all a lot of trouble, now, wouldn't it?

If you haven't guessed, meowing is our way of getting your attention. And it works, too. When we meow, you give us something, so we meow again. Who's got who trained around here, anyway?

Chattiest Kitty

And the winner is . . .

The prize for the chattiest kitty goes to the Siamese. They love to talk. Now we just have to figure out what they're saying!

Why do cats hiss?

You may think our meows and purrs are pleasant enough, but you won't enjoy our hisses! We don't blame you — when a cat hisses, that means we are *mad*! If we feel scared, we'll let out a big hiss to make ourselves seem threatening. So if you hear hissing, it means "Back up, buddy!" And if you see us arch our back and puff up our fur, that means we're *really* mad. (We think puffy fur makes us look bigger and meaner! Don't you agree?)

Why do cats scratch?

Sure, it's kind of fun to see you go bonkers when we sink our claws into your great-great-grandmother's heirloom rug. But we're not just being crazy cats. We have a real need to scratch things up.

- First of all, we have to keep fit. We need exercise, and what better way than to sink our claws in and s-t-r-e-t-c-h. It sure feels good!

- Next, we cats are fussy felines. We are very particular about good grooming. Scratching keeps our claws clean and sharp.

- Just like our big cousins, the tigers and the lions, we cats are territorial creatures. We scratch to leave our scent all over town. It lets the other cool cats know we've been around.

So if you want to save your furniture, take a tip from us: Set up a scratching post for your feline friends so we can safely claw to our hearts' content!

Cat claws are retractable. That means we can pull them in and out whenever we want. So watch out! You never know when we might get "cat scratch fever."

Why are cats' tongues so rough and scratchy?

We know our tongues feel like a piece of sandpaper. It's not our most appealing feature, but at least we don't leave you a drooling mess when we lick you, like dogs do. What's better? A kind coarse kiss, or sloppy slobbering saliva? We thought so. Score 1 for cats, 0 for dogs!

A cat's tongue is so rough because it has small spikes on it that we use to brush our fur. We also use our tongues to scrape meat off of bones. This is useful in the wild, but we house cats don't get too many meaty bones to chew. Call us wimpy, but these days we prefer our meat from a can.

Why do cats lick themselves?

Well, if you must know . . .

🐱 We use our tongues to wash ourselves. Sure, a bar of soap might work just as well, but then we would have to take a — *gulp* — bath. We think a bit of fur on our tongues beats getting wet any day.

🐱 Call us fussy felines, but we like our fur coats fluffy. Licking our coat fluffs up our fur.

🐱 On those really hot dog — or cat — days of summer, we lick ourselves to stay cool. It's like a built-in air conditioner — and we save on energy bills, too!

🐱 We use our tongues to clean a scratch or cut.

By cleaning ourselves with our own saliva, we're able to spread our scent around whenever we brush up against something. Isn't that thoughtful?

Feline Fact

The two places a cat can't lick are the face and the head. Want to know our nifty solution? Washcloth paws! We lick our paw, then clean our face and head with it.

Why do cats push at you with their paws?

When we push at you with our paws, we're not telling you to move over. We're trying to tell you that we like you . . . a lot! In fact, you remind us of our moms. When we were kittens, we would get milk to drink from our mom by kneading her with our paws. And when we do this to our people friends, it means we're feeling calm and relaxed, just like we did when we were small. So we're not being pushy — we're just being happy cats!

No Re-gifting, Please!

Cats bring their owners dead mice or other small animals to be friendly. It's a present for you! Pretty thoughtful of us, wouldn't you say?

Do cats always land on their feet?

Just call me *Supercat:* Able to leap from tall buildings in a single bound! Well, that isn't exactly true. Buildings might be a bit high, but we cats are able to fall from trees or housetops gracefully. When we fall from up high, our body rotates in the air before we touch the ground. That way we always land on our feet, instead of on our back or head. Because that would hurt . . . a lot!

The Tail End of Things

Our tail is an important part of our balancing act. It helps keep us steady while we walk.

Do Cats Really Have 9 Lives?

No, we're not supernatural. But because of our great balance and our ability to fall on our feet, we're able to survive some pretty tricky situations that other animals might not. But you can call us Supercats, anyway. We like the way that sounds.

Why do cats wag their tails?

We cats are complex creatures. Even our tail movement can mean different things!

- If we wave our tail, that means something might be bothering us. We'll leave you guessing as to what it might be . . . and, of course, we expect you to attend to it right away.

- If our tail begins to wag faster, that means we're mad. Did you forget our cat food again?

- If our tail twitches or quivers, that means we're excited. But don't expect us to do any tricks for you.

Missing Cattail?

The Manx is the only cat that doesn't really have a tail. Although many are born tailless, some Manx cats are born with a slight stump.

A Tall Tail

Talk about cat pride . . . domestic cats can hold their heads — and tails — high! We're the only member of the cat family able to hold our tail upright when we walk. Wild cats hold their tails down or level with the ground.

Why do cats sleep so much?

Sleeping is our favorite thing to do. And we do it so well that they even named a nap after us! Some might call us lazy. But by nature we cats are hunters, and we need a lot of rest to be good hunters. In the wild, our cousins might sleep all day to save their strength to hunt at night when it's not so hot. But what's *our* excuse? Well, we don't really have one. We just like to nap.

Cats can sleep up to 16 hours a day — or more! But only a third of that time is spent in a true deep sleep. The rest of the time we're just taking a catnap, with one eye half open. We still like to keep an eye on things, so don't try any funny stuff!

Night Owls . . . Er, Cats

Cats are nocturnal. That means we like to sleep all day but become party animals at night. When you want a little shut-eye, we want to play, play, play! Mouse toy, anyone?

Why do cats rub up against people's legs?

Because we like you! It may seem funny, but we like things better when they smell like us. We rub up against you to leave our scent on you. We think you smell much sweeter that way.

All cats are territorial. We leave our mark by scratching, spraying, and rubbing against things with our scent. It's our way of telling other cats, "Hey, this is my spot. Stay away!"

Feline Friends

When cats rub their noses together, they're often letting each other know they're friends.

Why do cats shed their fur?

What do you mean, you don't like matted feline fur all over your house? Ever try swallowing it? *Plbhtht!* We cats sure do have a lot of fur to deal with. And some of us more than others. Our cat family is divided into three types: short-haired, long-haired, and hairless. But no matter how much of it we have — or don't have — we all shed. It helps us to regulate our body temperature.

Fur Coat Fever

- The Maine Coon is one of the furriest cats. Its thick fur coat helps it stay warm during chilly winters.

- The prize for the curliest cat goes to the Curly-Haired Devon Rex cat. Every hair on its body is curly — even its whiskers!

- Cute and cuddly aren't the first words that come to mind to describe the "hairless" Sphynx. But remember, beauty is only fur deep. This not-so-pretty kitty isn't really hairless. It actually has a thin layer of fur.

And *Fur*-thermore . . .

You can help us cats shed some of our fur by brushing us often. But no ribbons and bows, please.

Why do cats eat grass?

We know it makes you humans happy to feed us finicky felines some of the fanciest food money can buy. So doesn't it just make you mad when you see us eating plain old grass from your backyard instead? Well, we cats have our reasons why we like to go green once in a while:

- It aids our digestion. Think of it as a kitty after-dinner mint.

- It helps get rid of some of those hair balls we have in our stomachs from all that fur cleaning we do. And we get to leave a nice surprise for you to pick up — aren't we thoughtful?

- Some folks say it's a good source of folic acid, something our cat bodies need.

So don't be offended the next time we turn up our noses at your fancy foods and opt for lawn lunch instead. Grass is good for us!

A Little Nip

Some cats just love catnip. We love the way it smells and we love to sniff it, lick it, and roll all around in it. If you want your cat to think you're *purr*-fect, get her some catnip-filled toys to play with.

Houseplant Hazards

Cats may love grass, but not all plants are good for us. Keep your cat away from your household plants. Many of them are poisonous for us to eat.

Why do cats climb trees?

Sure, life is pretty good for us cats on land. So why would we want to mess things up and get ourselves stuck in a tree? Well, there are a lot of reasons we cats crawl upward. Here are a few:

🐱 For protection. That crazy dog from next door chasing us can never catch us if we're hiding in a tree.

🐱 For a "pouncing perch." We get a good *cat's*-eye view of things from up high. It's a great place to just sit and watch the world go by . . . or to view other unsuspecting animals down below.

Feline Fact

The leopard is the largest tree-climbing cat. I wouldn't want to look up and find that cat napping in my apple tree, would you?

Why are cats so good at EVERYTHING?

Okay, we admit it. We asked this question ourselves. We are superior in so many ways, we thought it was only fair of us to let you know how and why.

Our Superior Sense of Smell . . .
Once we get a whiff of a scent, we might remember it for the rest of our lives. That's great if it smells like fish, not so great if it smells like dirty socks.

. . . and Sight . . .
We can see at night a lot better than both dogs and humans. That's because our eyes have an extra layer of cells that work like a mirror to reflect light. This helps us hunt at night, which leaves plenty of time during the day for what we do best — nap!